This Coloring book Belongs to:

_____

CopyRights 2020 Papa Abdou Books, Authour, Illustrator, or Publishing info.

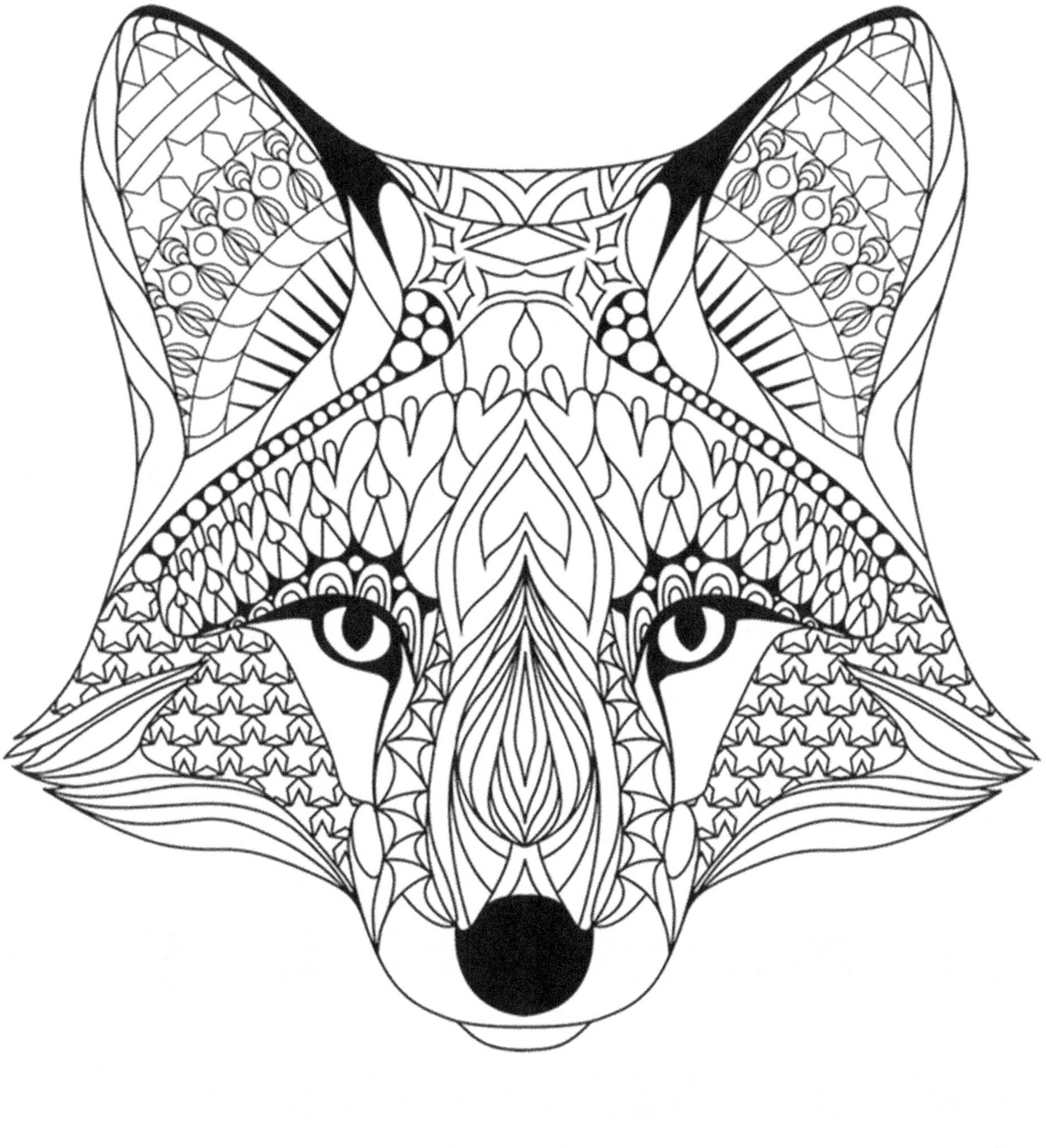

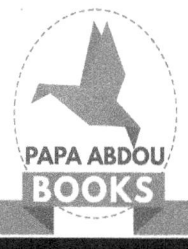

CopyRights 2020 Papa Abdou Books, Authour, Illustrator, or Publishing info.

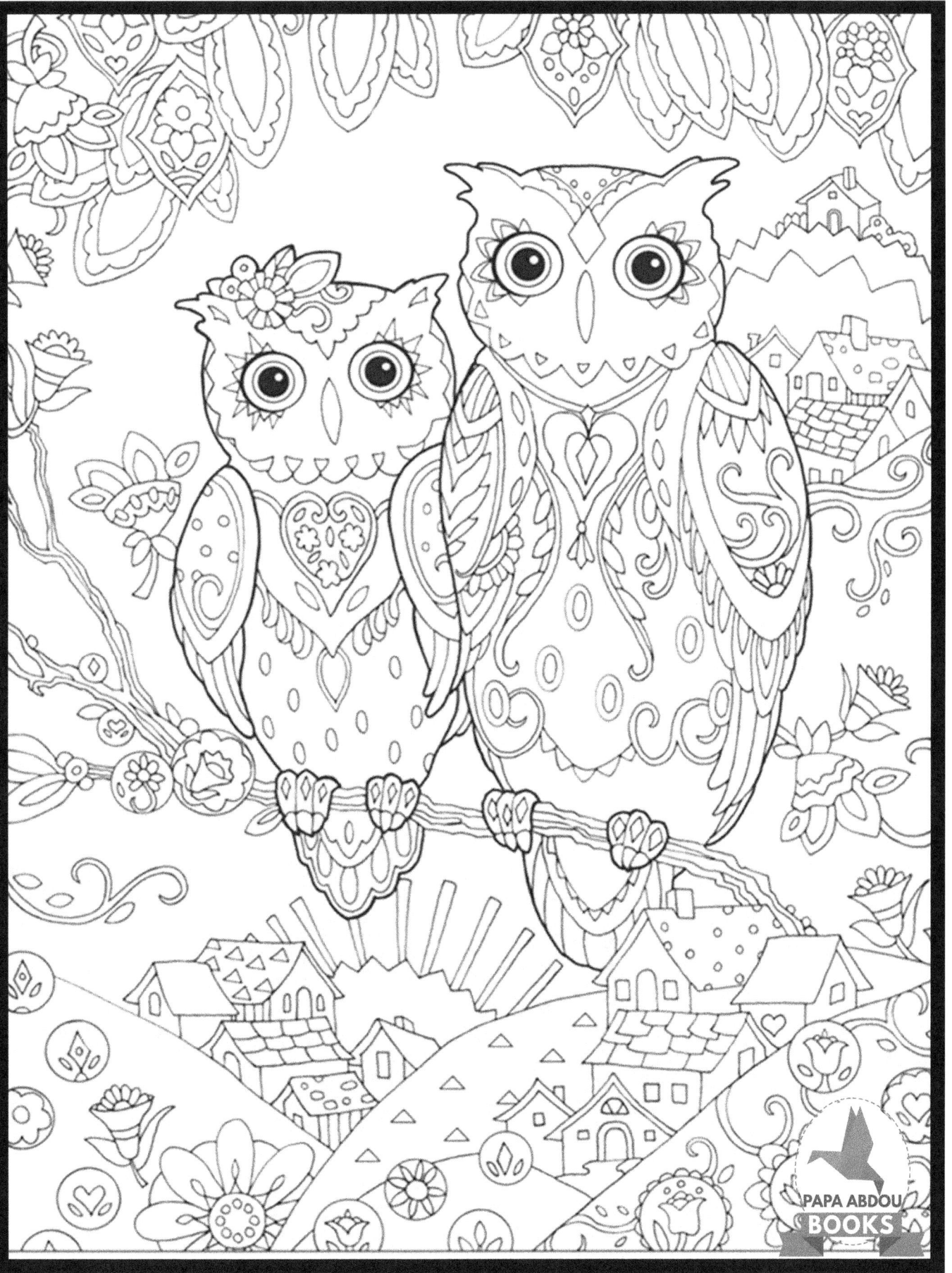

CopyRights 2020 Papa Abdou Books, Authour, Illustrator, or Publishing info.

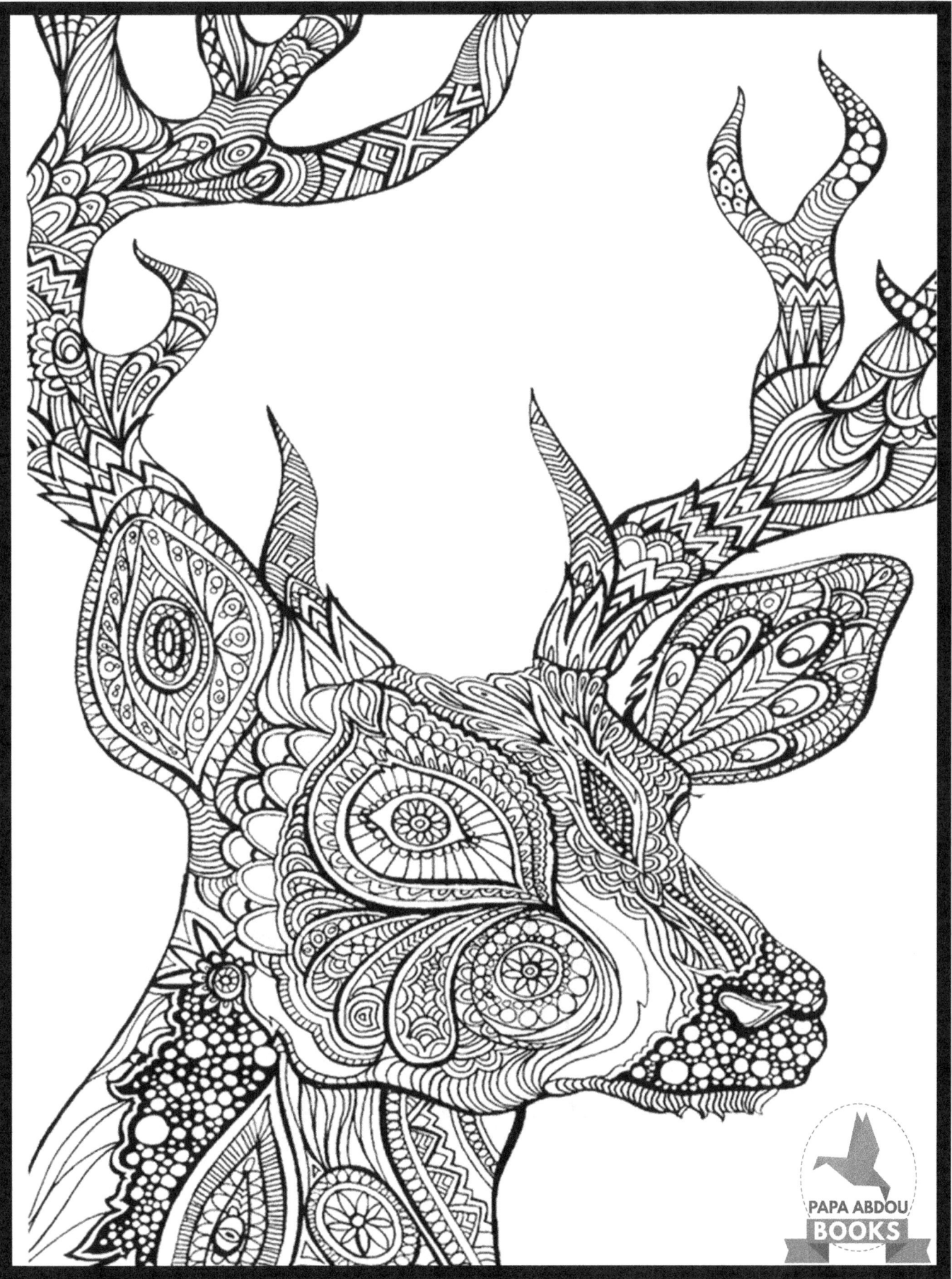

CopyRights 2020 Papa Abdou Books, Authour, Illustrator, or Publishing info.

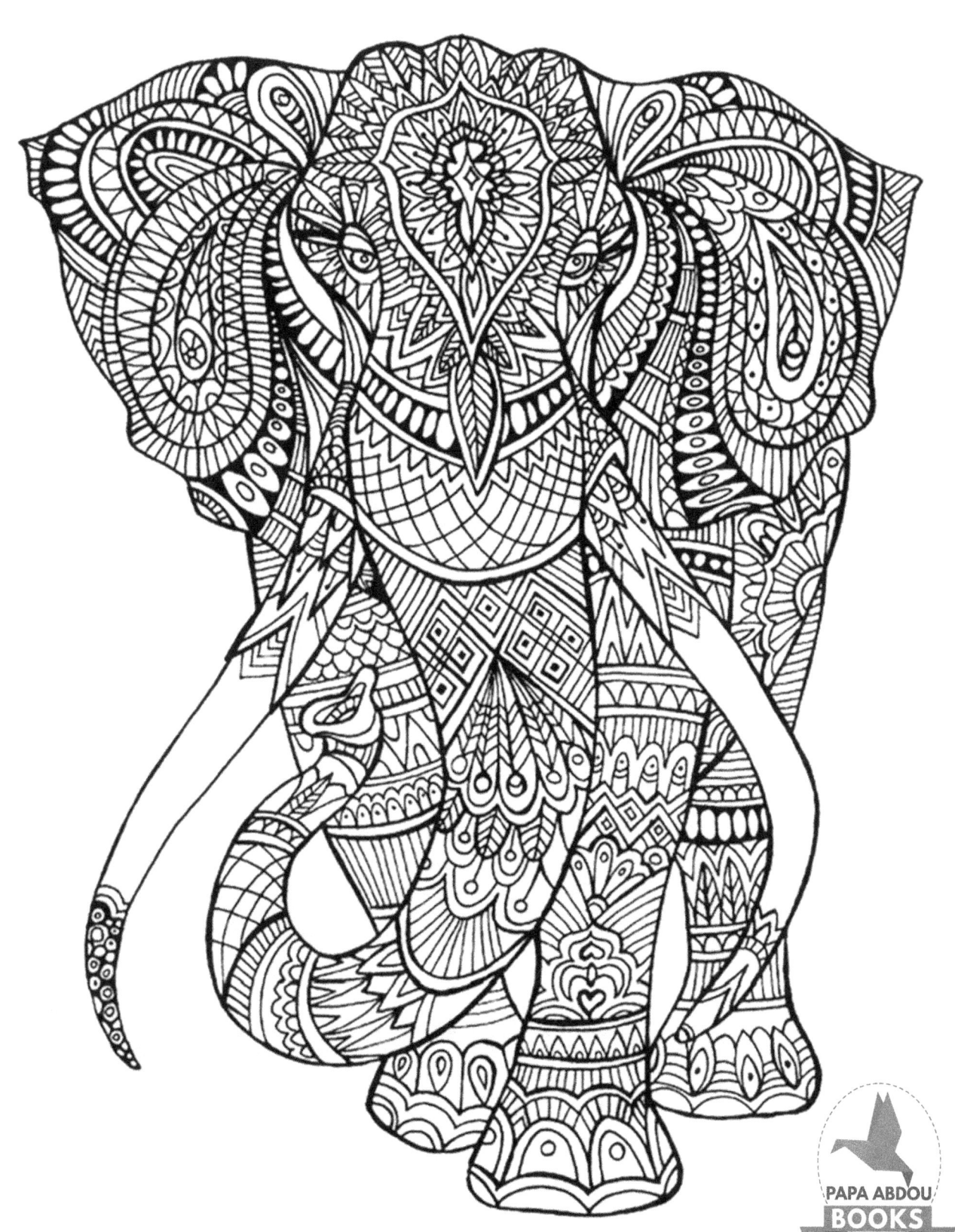

CopyRights 2020 Papa Abdou Books, Authour, Illustrator, or Publishing info.

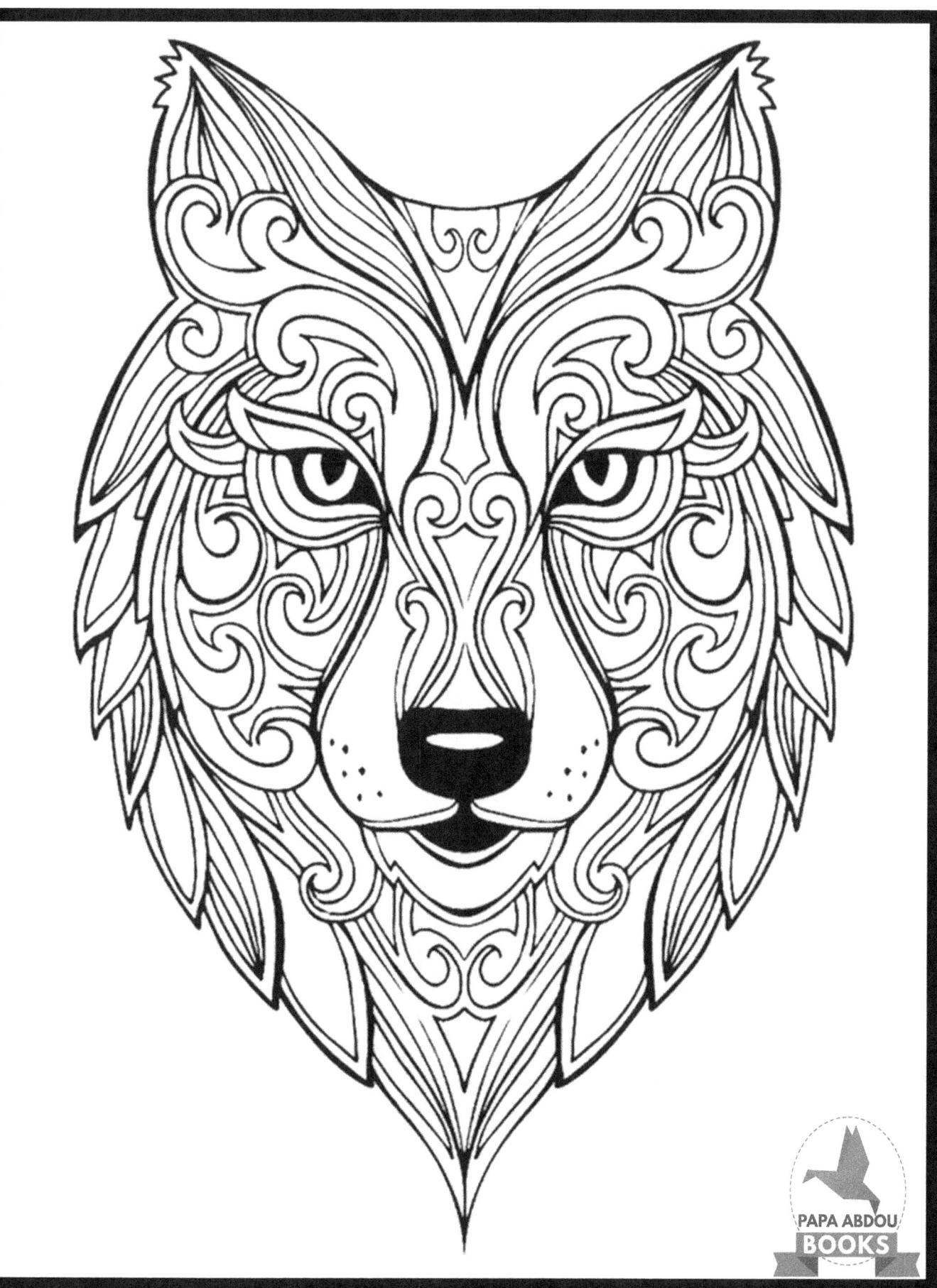

CopyRights 2020 Papa Abdou Books, Authour, Illustrator, or Publishing info.

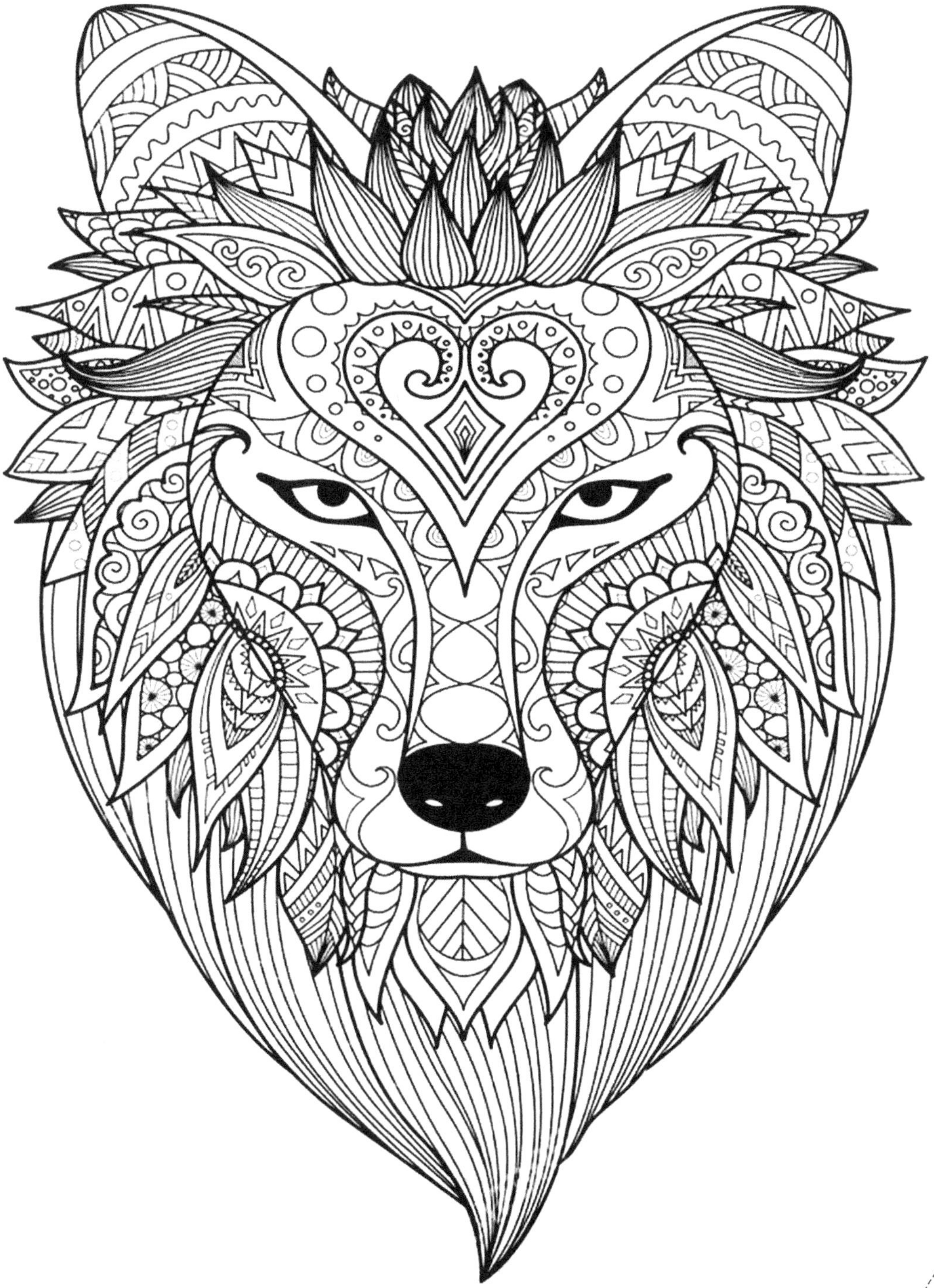

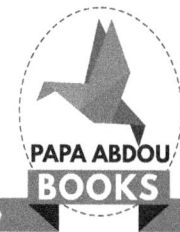

CopyRights 2020 Papa Abdou Books, Authour, Illustrator, or Publishing info.

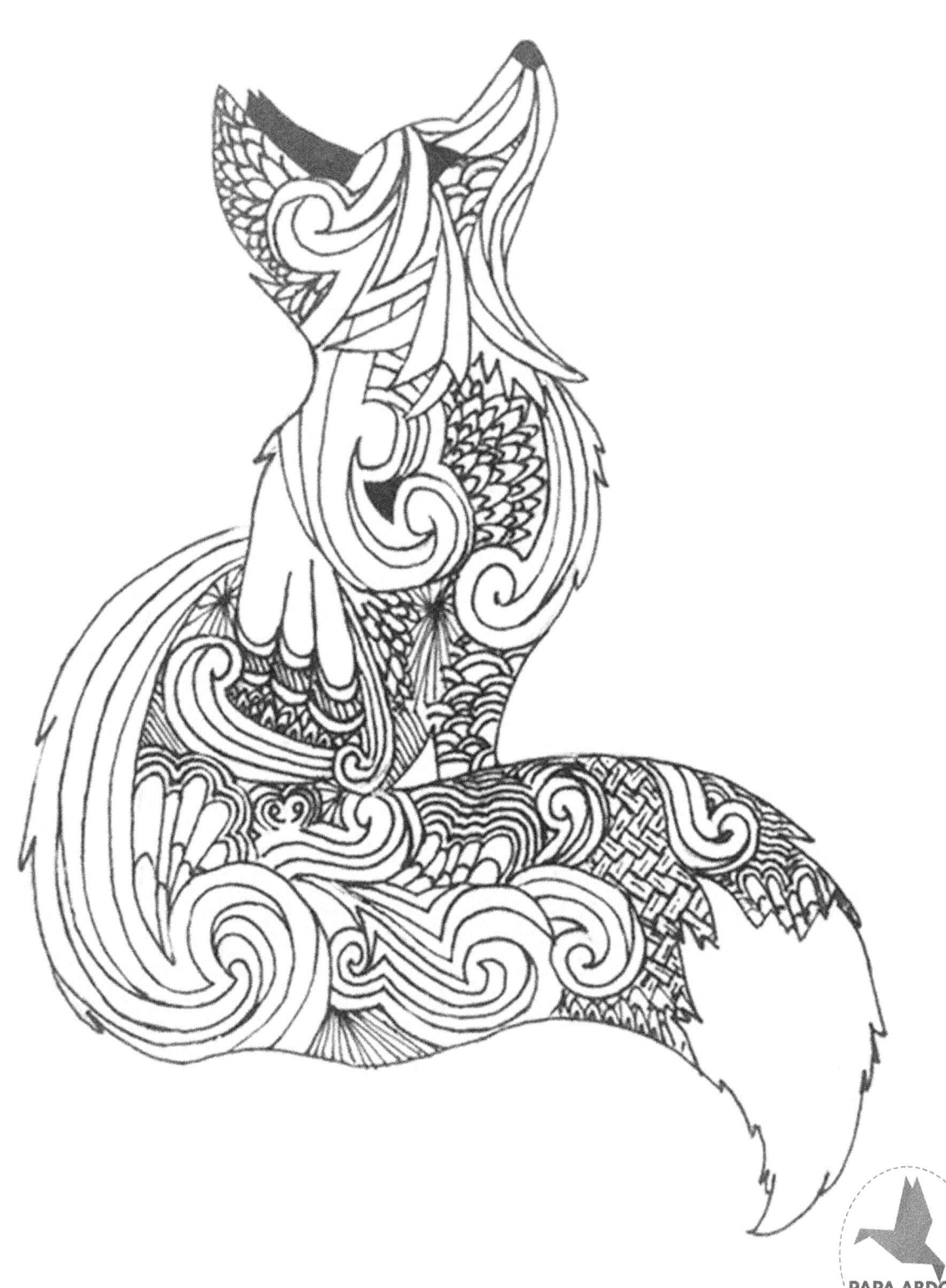

CopyRights 2020 Papa Abdou Books, Authour, Illustrator, or Publishing info.

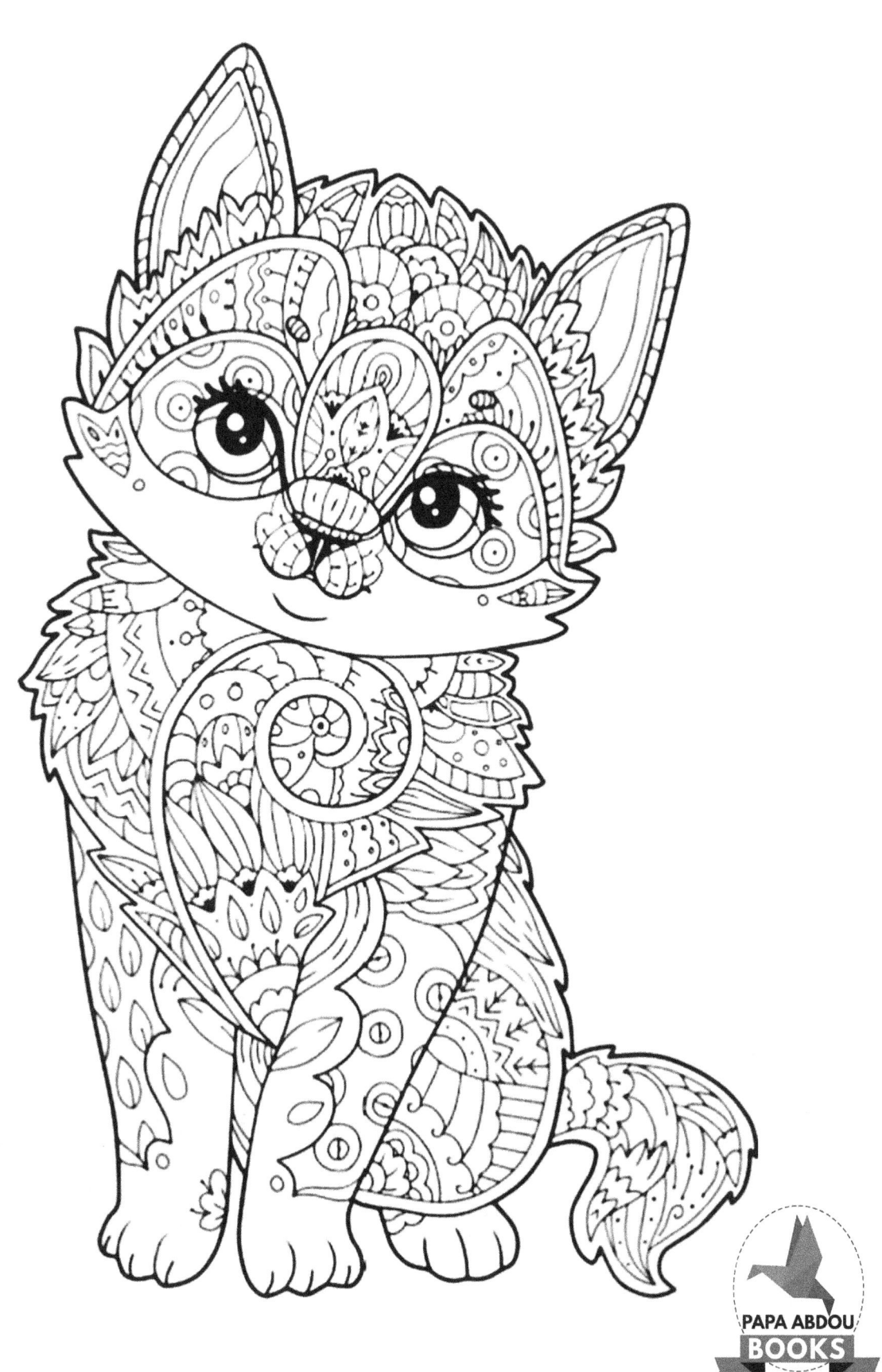

CopyRights 2020 Papa Abdou Books, Authour, Illustrator, or Publishing info.

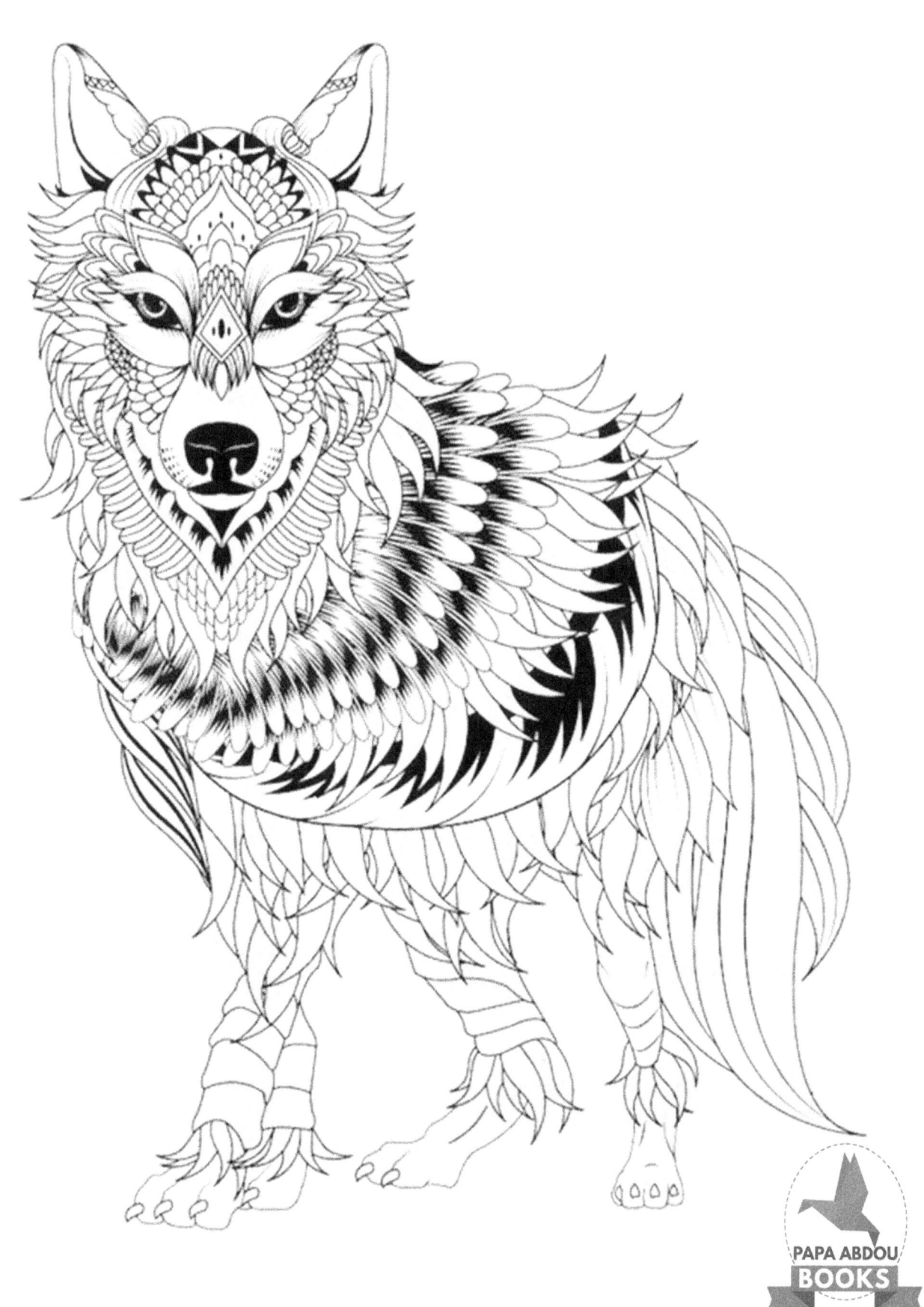

CopyRights 2020 Papa Abdou Books, Authour, Illustrator, or Publishing info.

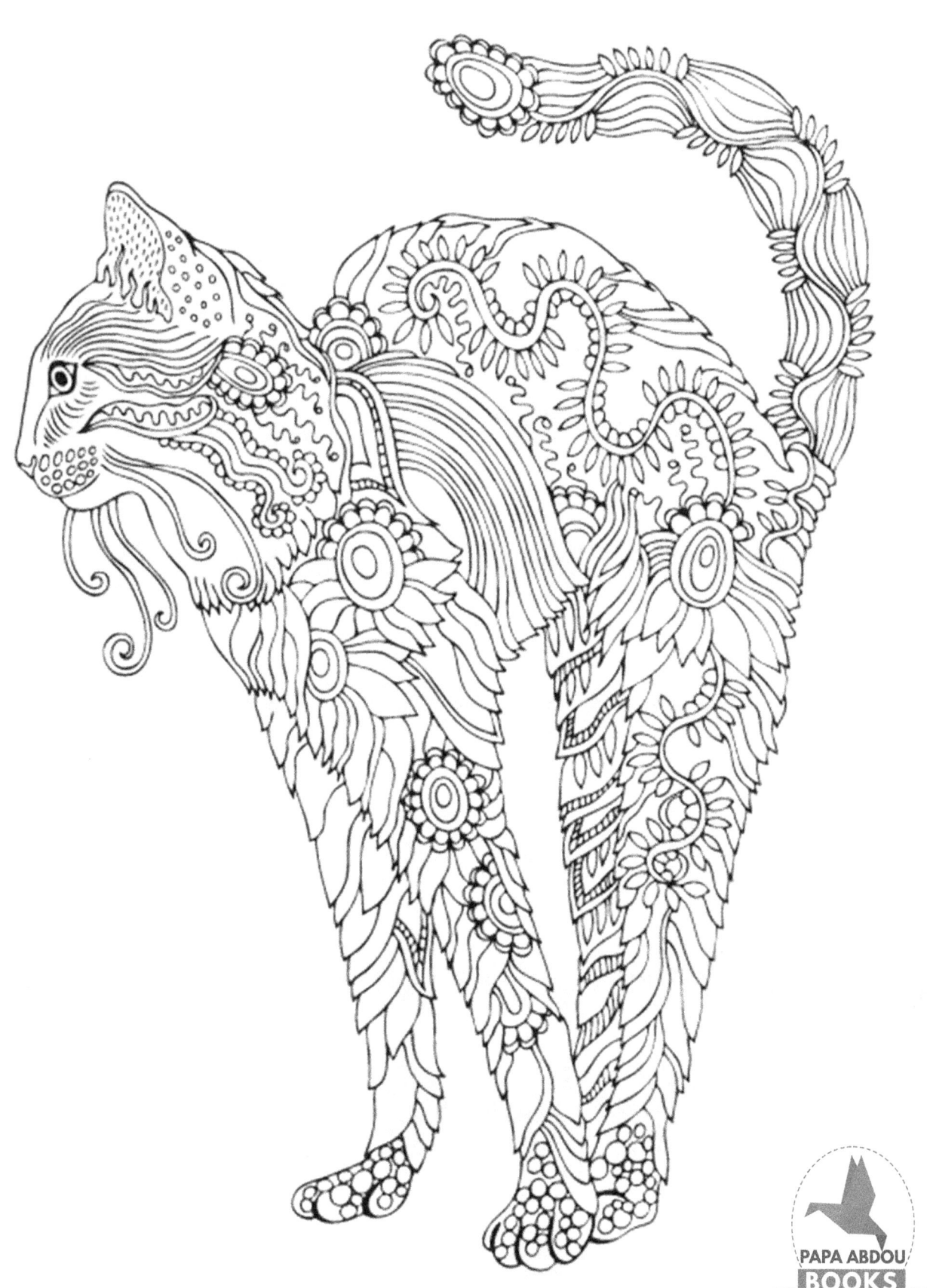

CopyRights 2020 Papa Abdou Books, Authour, Illustrator, or Publishing info.

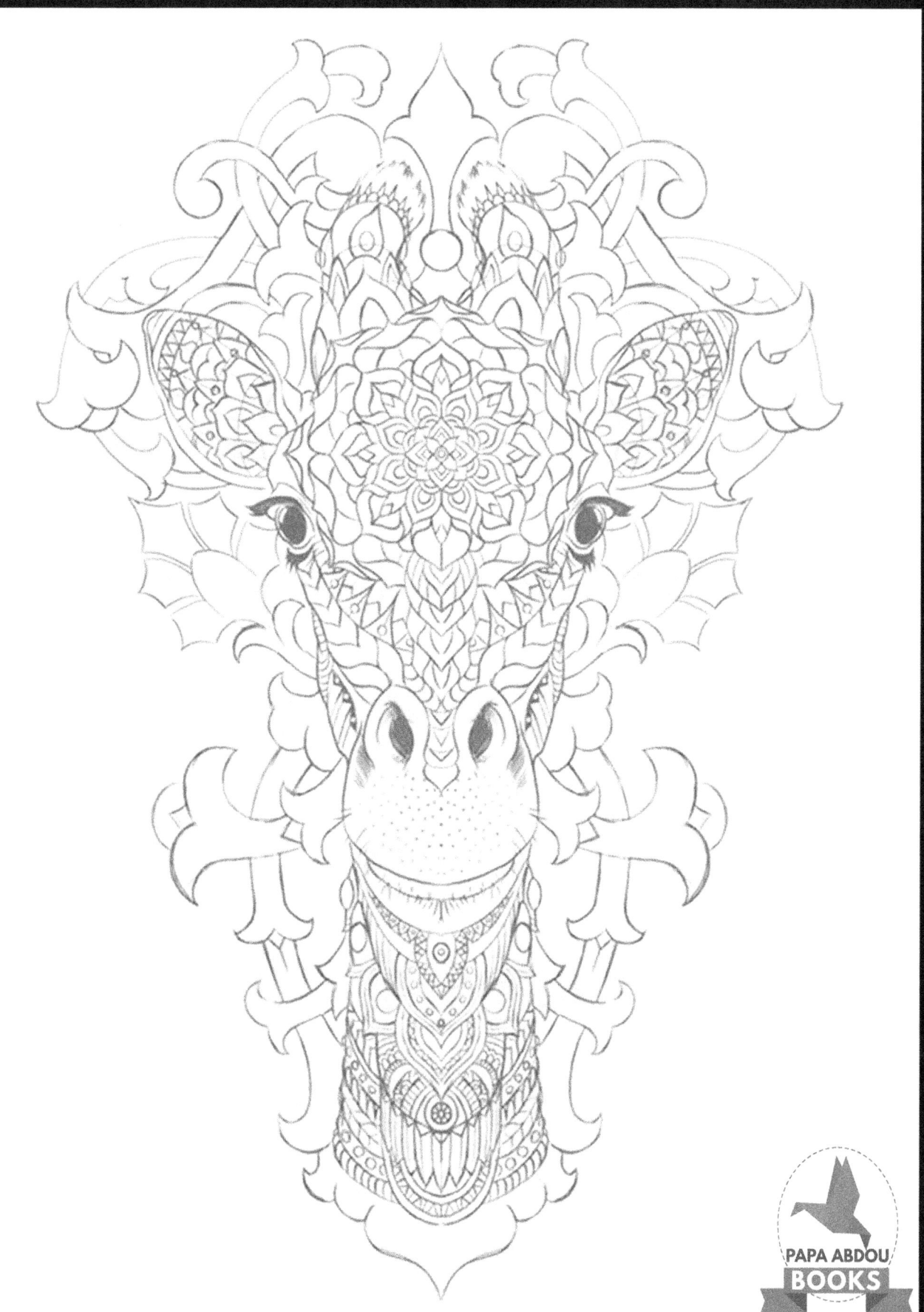

CopyRights 2020 Papa Abdou Books, Authour, Illustrator, or Publishing info.

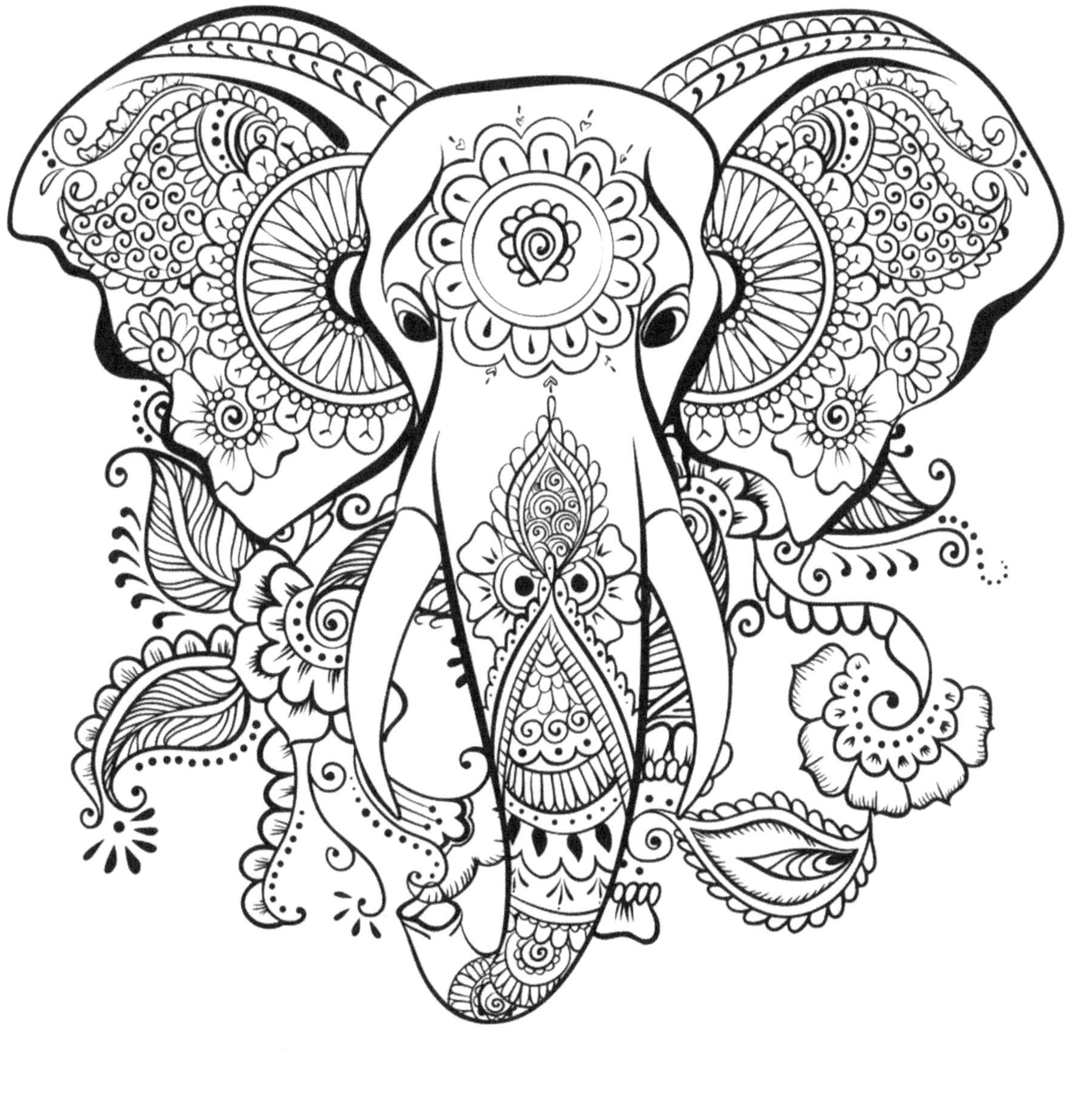

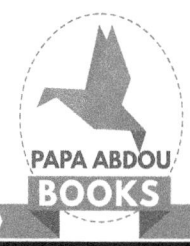

CopyRights 2020 Papa Abdou Books, Authour, Illustrator, or Publishing info.

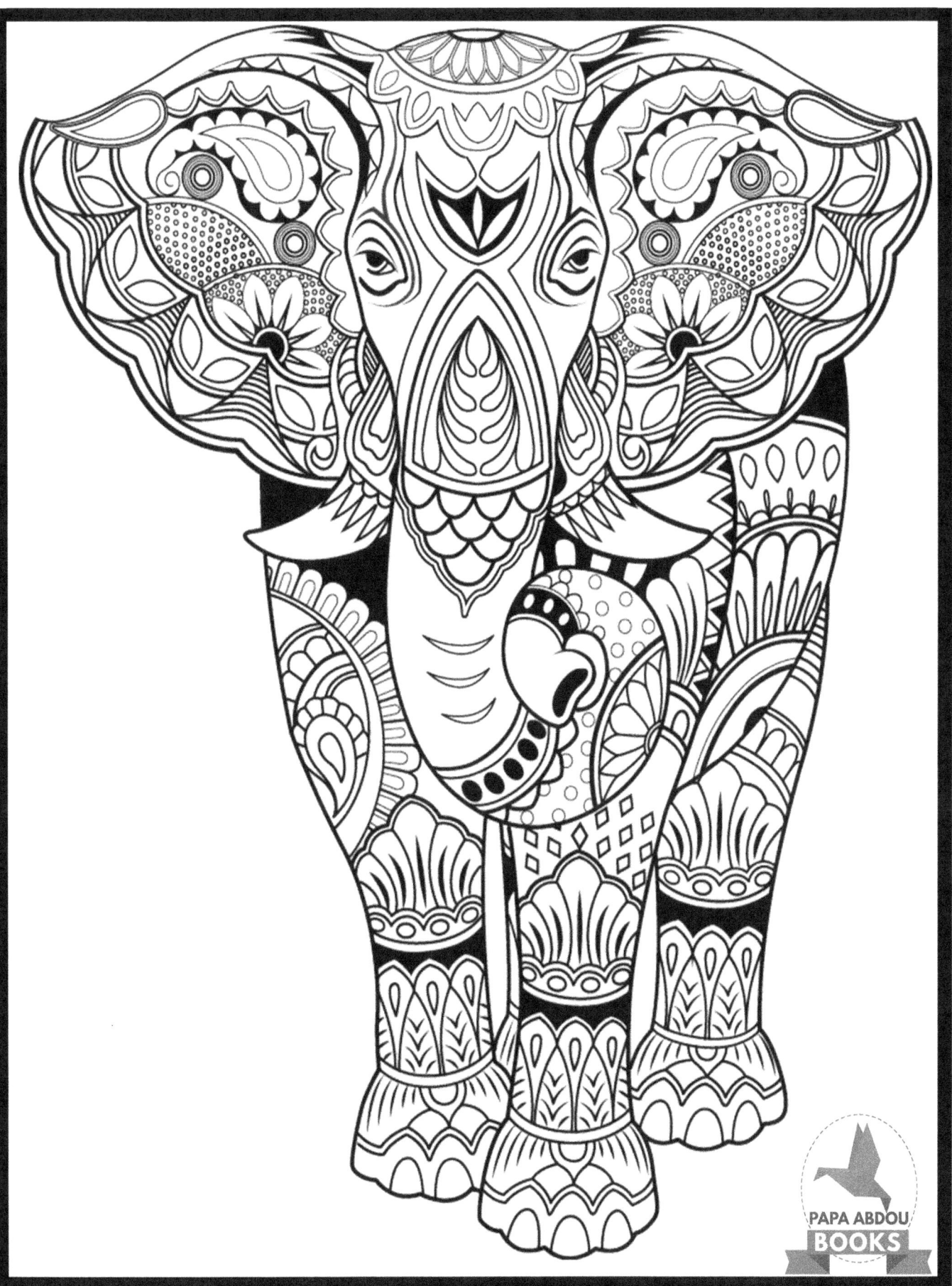

CopyRights 2020 Papa Abdou Books, Authour, Illustrator, or Publishing info.

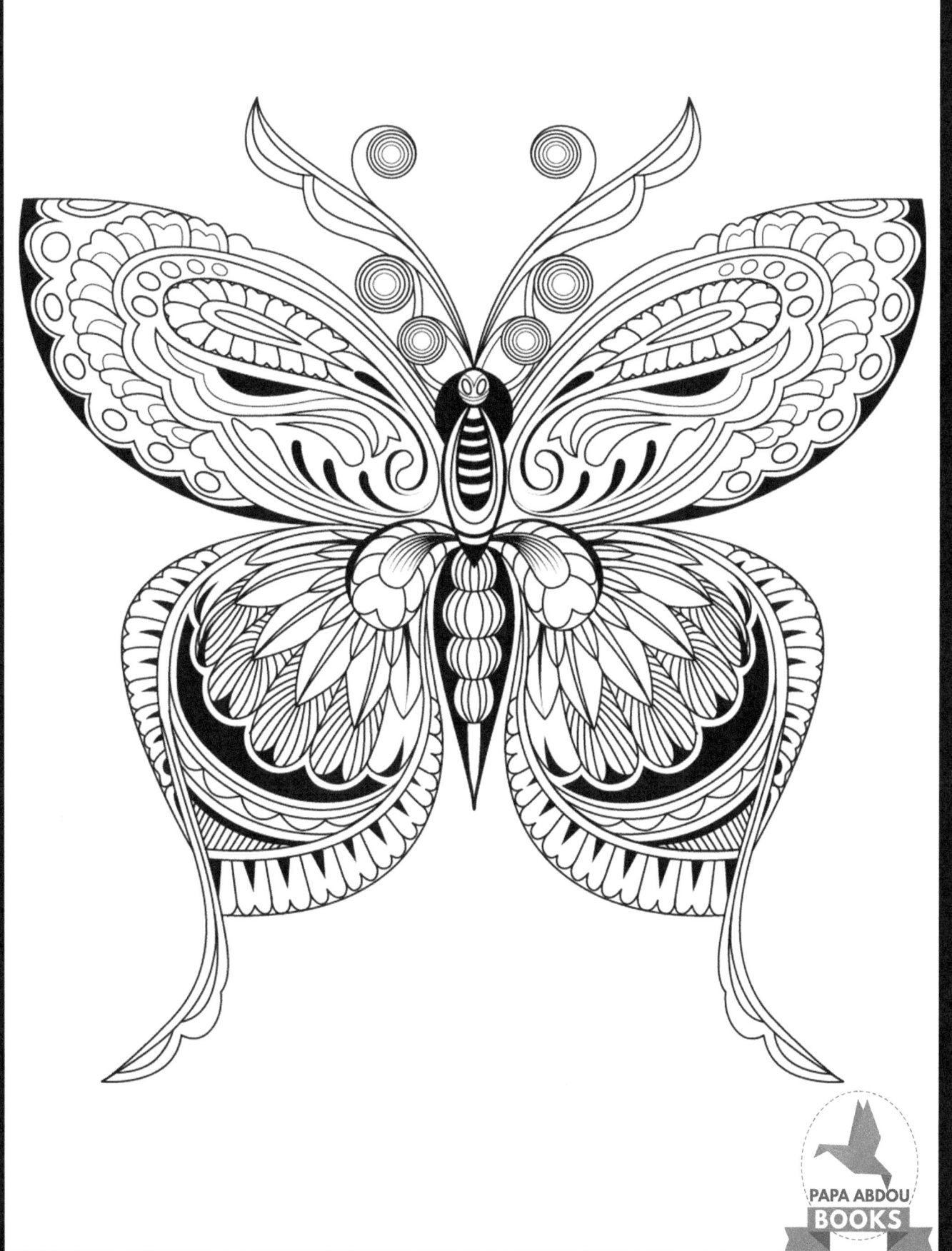

CopyRights 2020 Papa Abdou Books, Authour, Illustrator, or Publishing info.

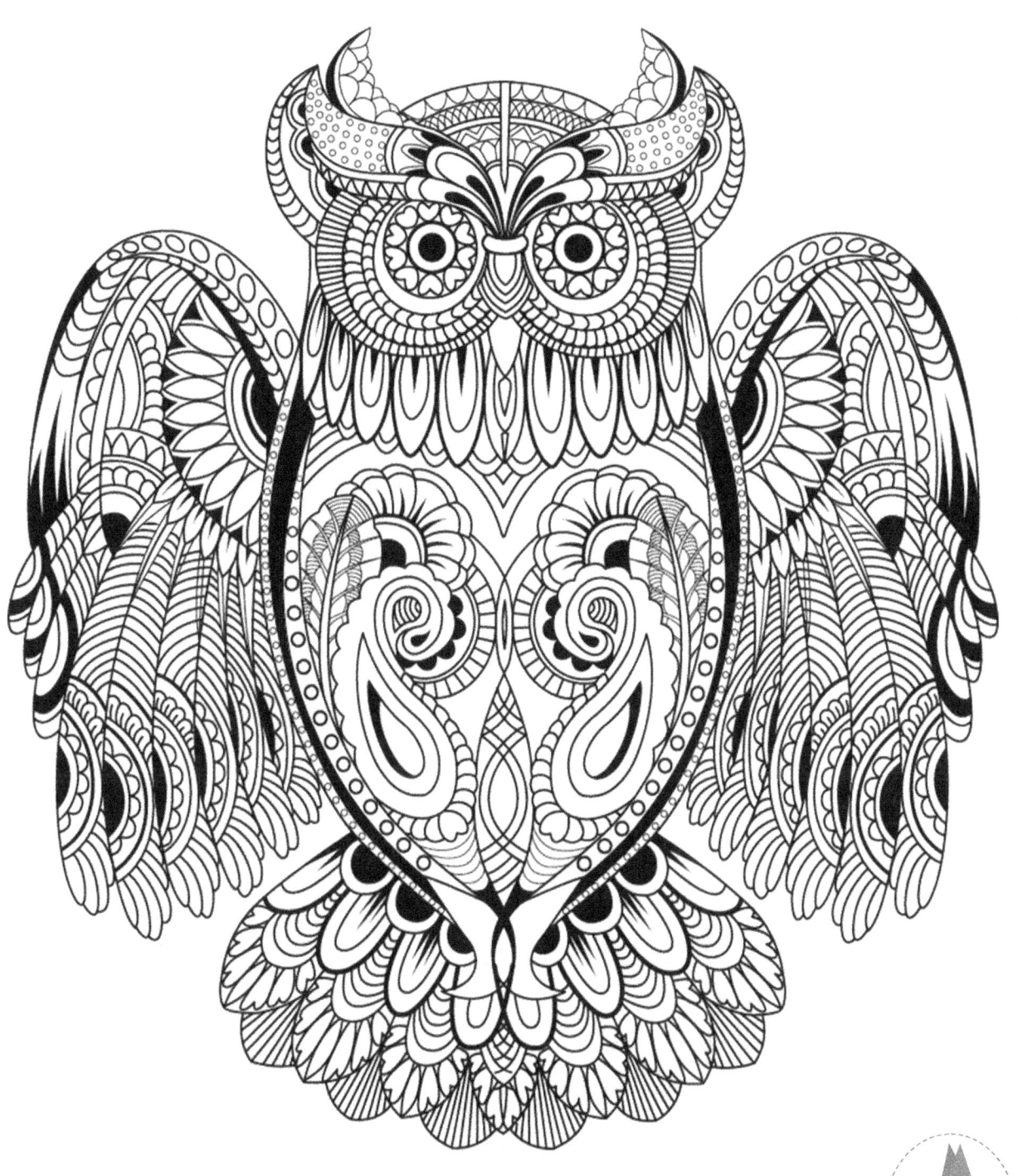

CopyRights 2020 Papa Abdou Books, Authour, Illustrator, or Publishing info.

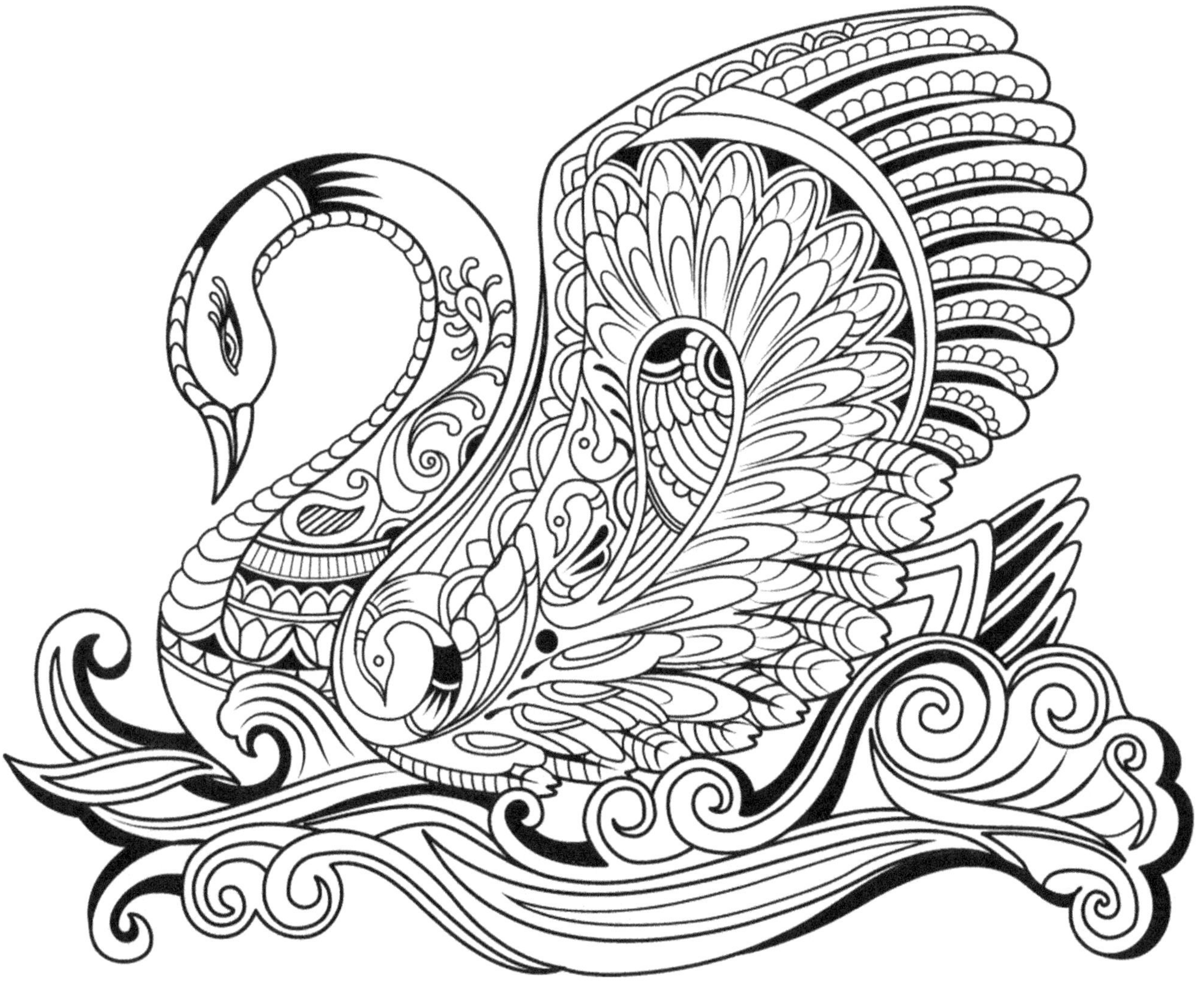

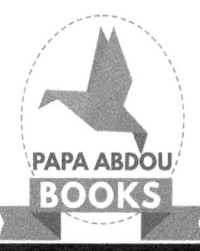

CopyRights 2020 Papa Abdou Books, Authour, Illustrator, or Publishing info.

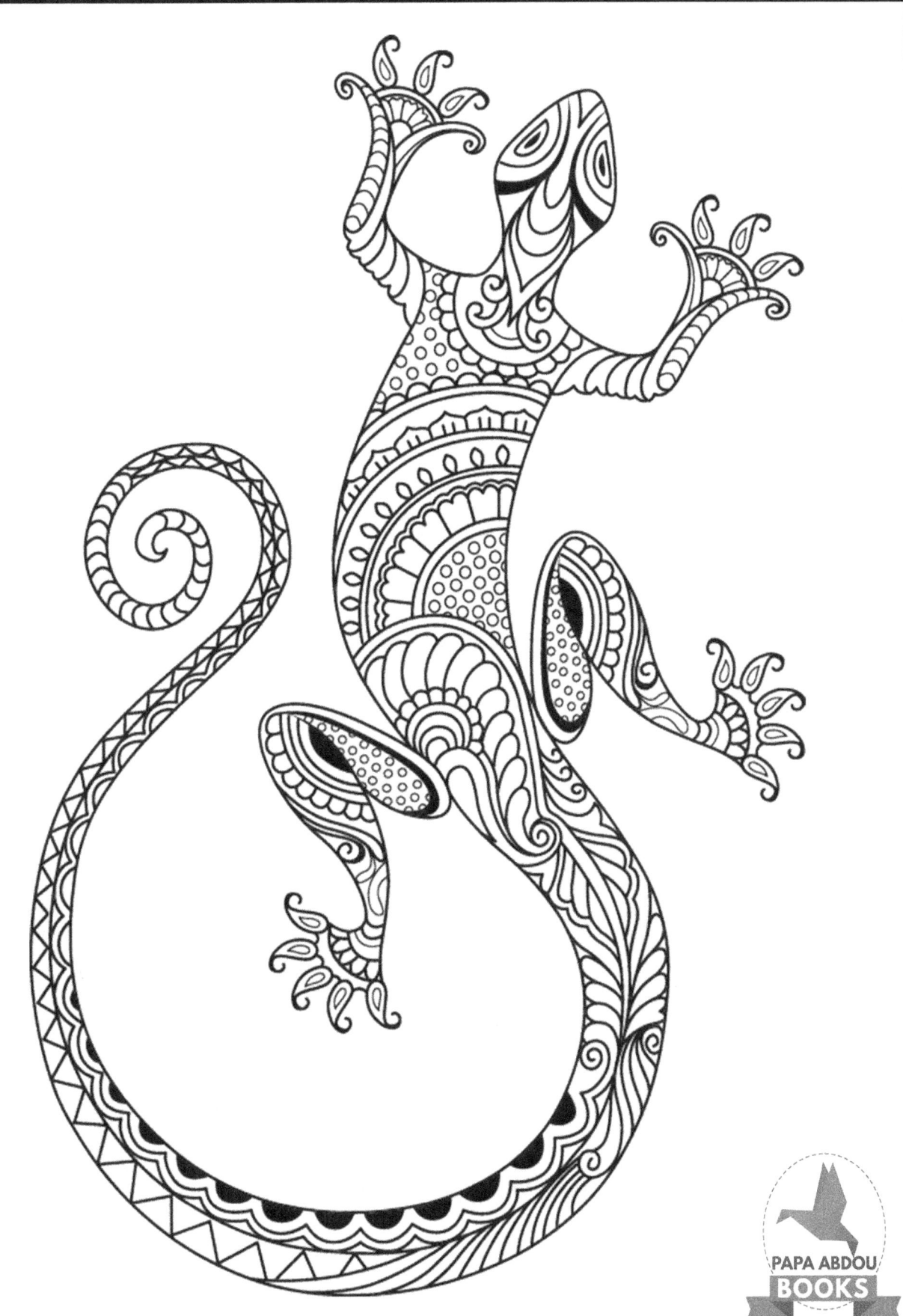

CopyRights 2020 Papa Abdou Books, Authour, Illustrator, or Publishing info.

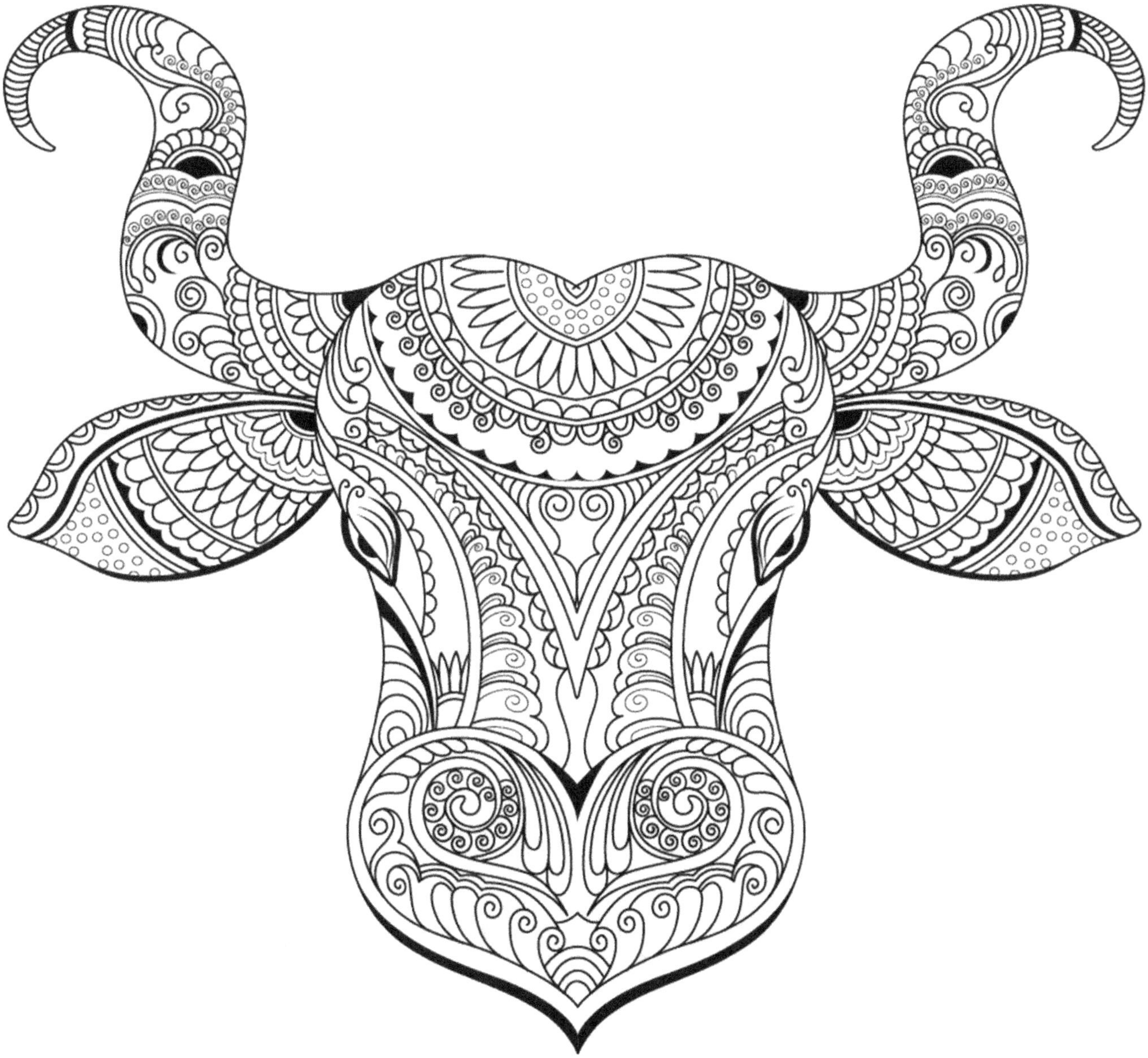

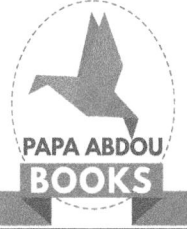

CopyRights 2020 Papa Abdou Books, Authour, Illustrator, or Publishing info.

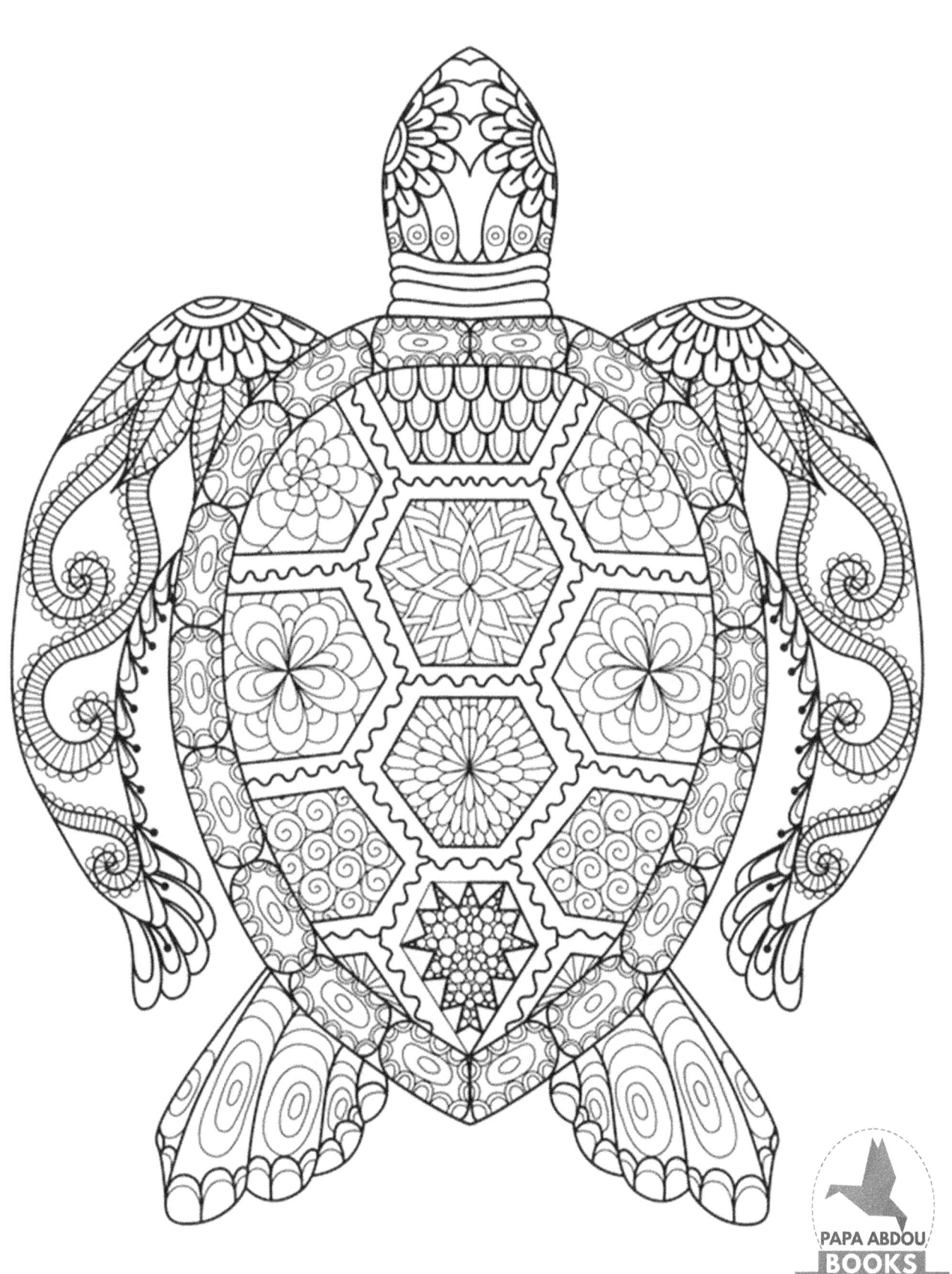

CopyRights 2020 Papa Abdou Books, Authour, Illustrator, or Publishing info.

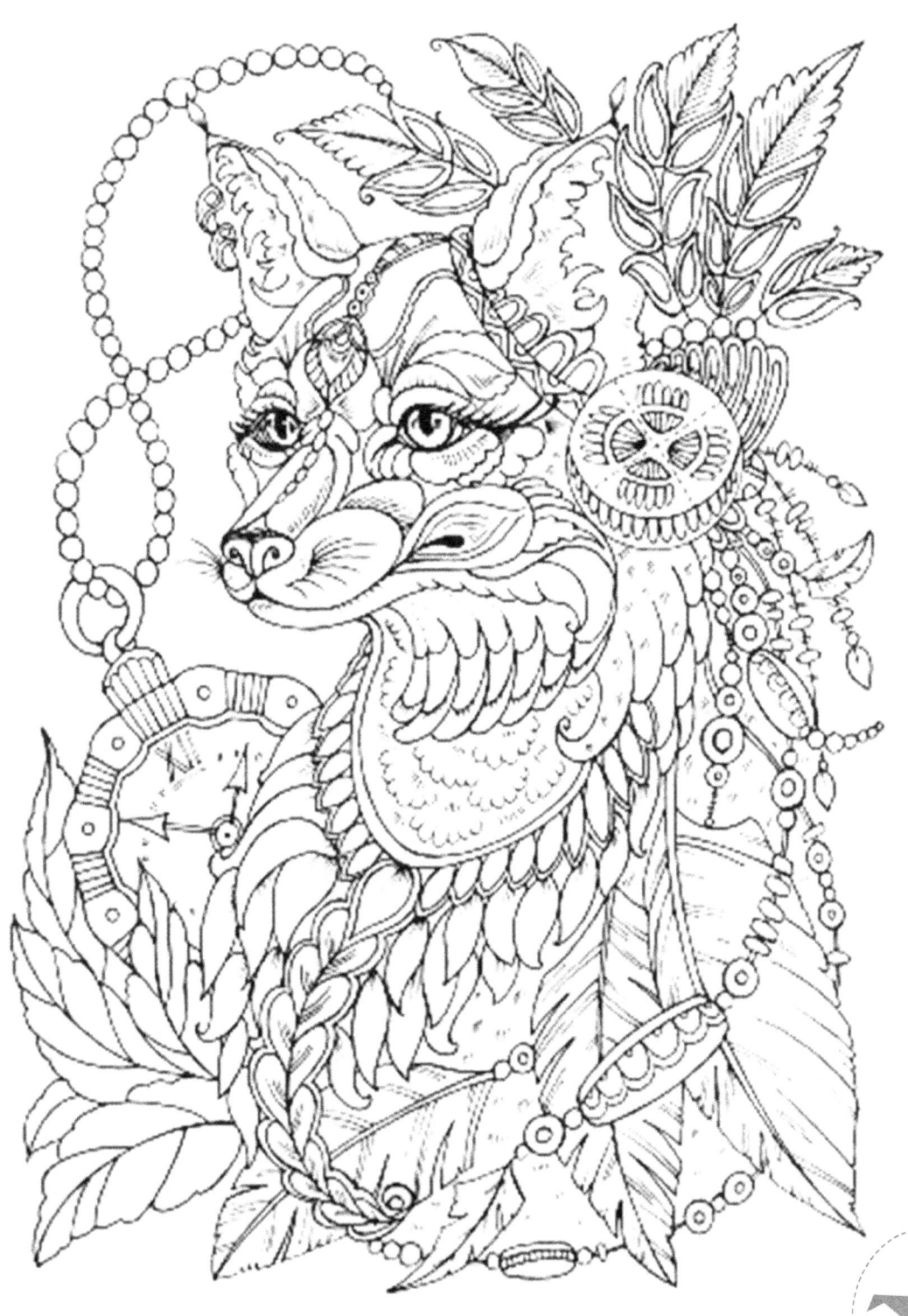

CopyRights 2020 Papa Abdou Books, Authour, Illustrator, or Publishing info.

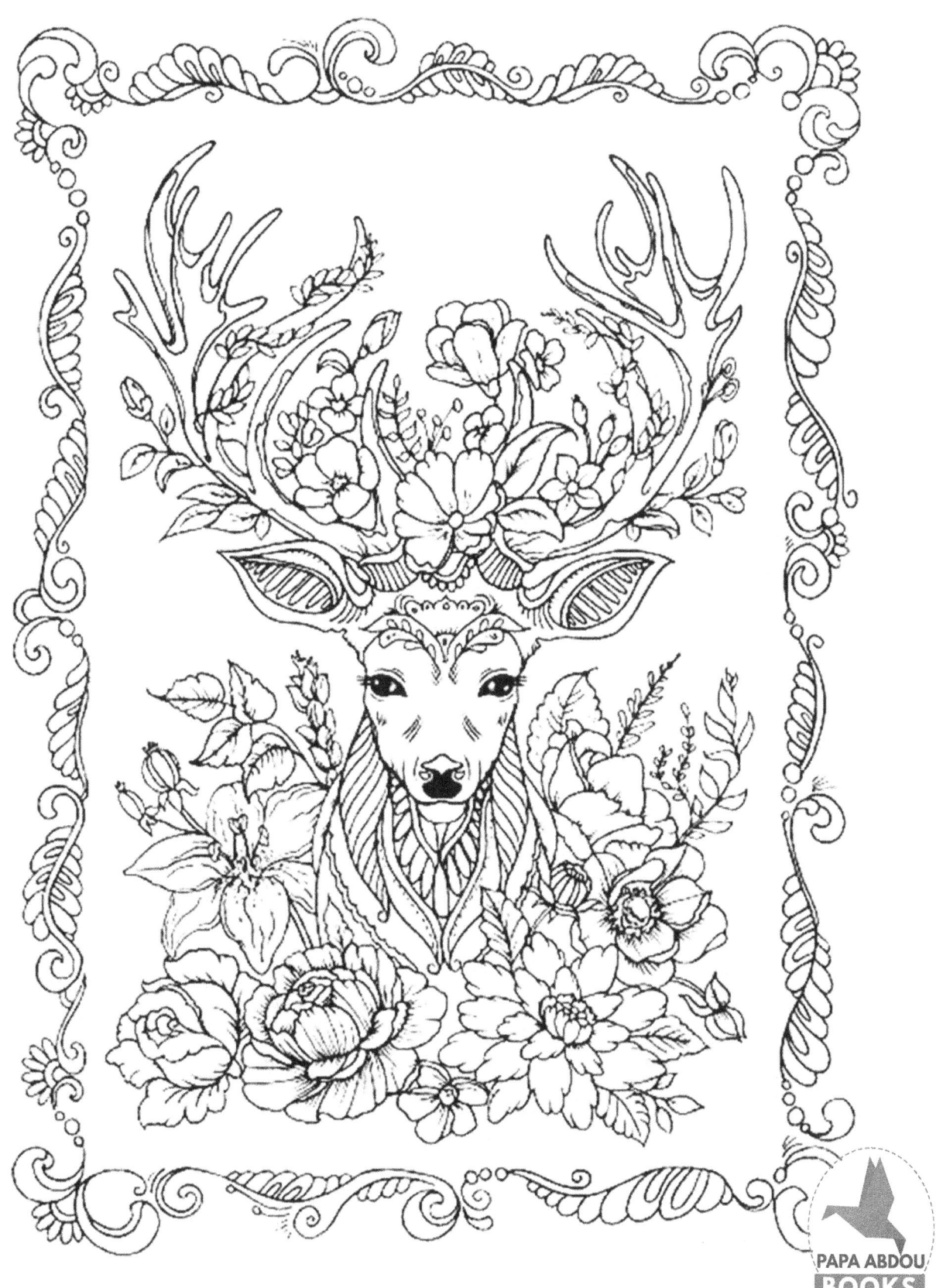

CopyRights 2020 Papa Abdou Books, Authour, Illustrator, or Publishing info.

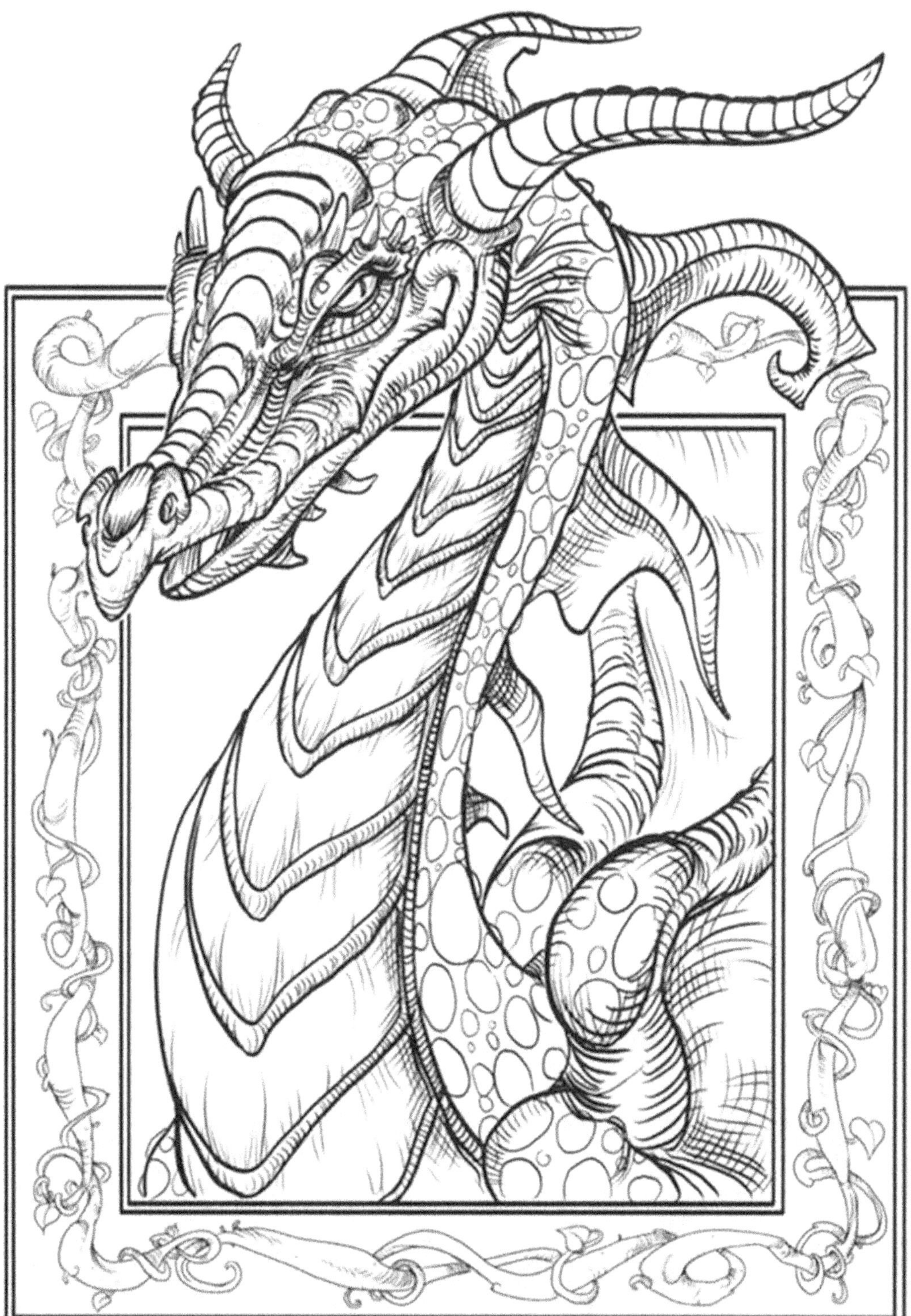

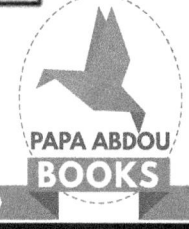

CopyRights 2020 Papa Abdou Books, Authour, Illustrator, or Publishing info.

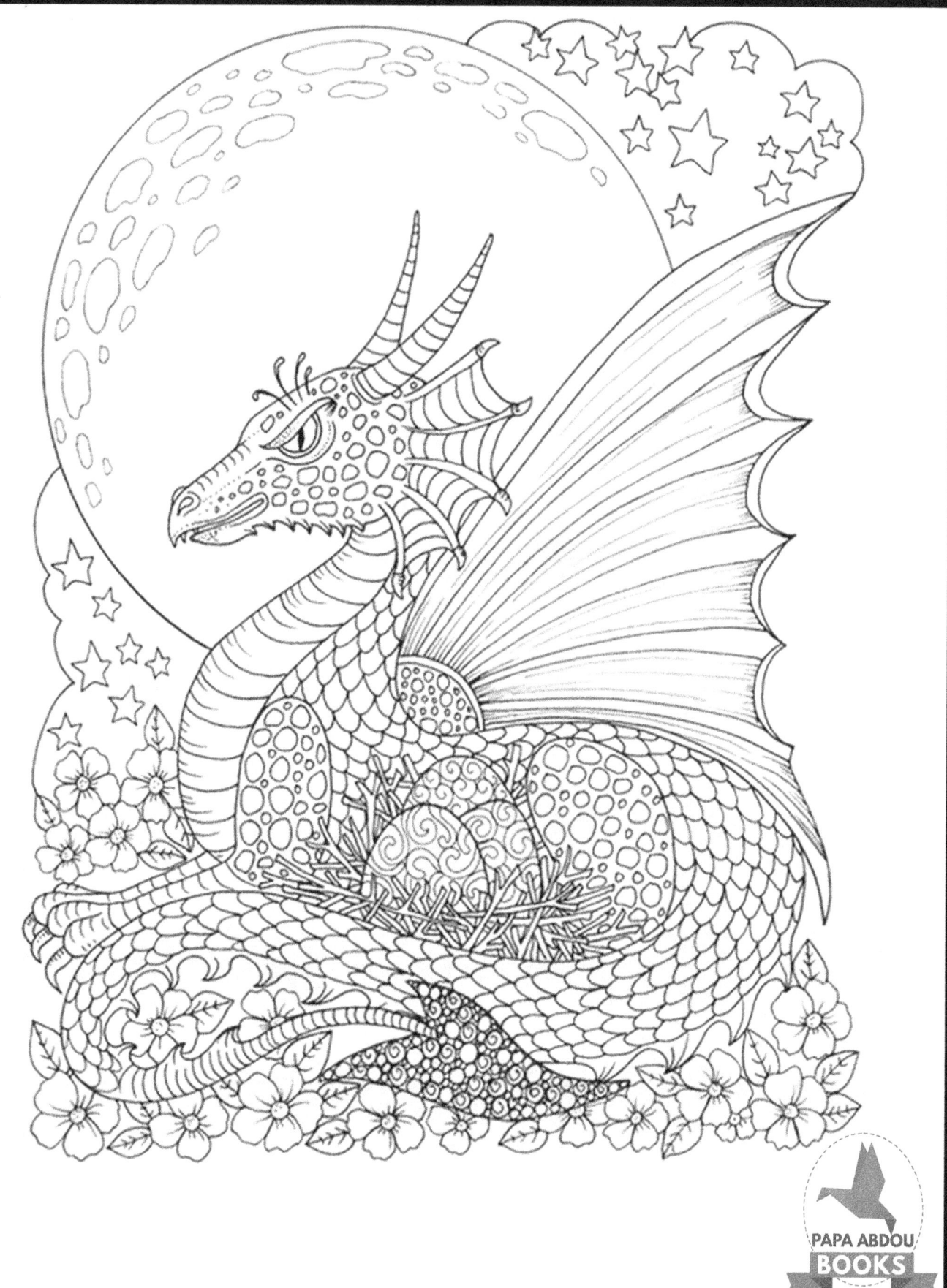

CopyRights 2020 Papa Abdou Books, Authour, Illustrator, or Publishing info.

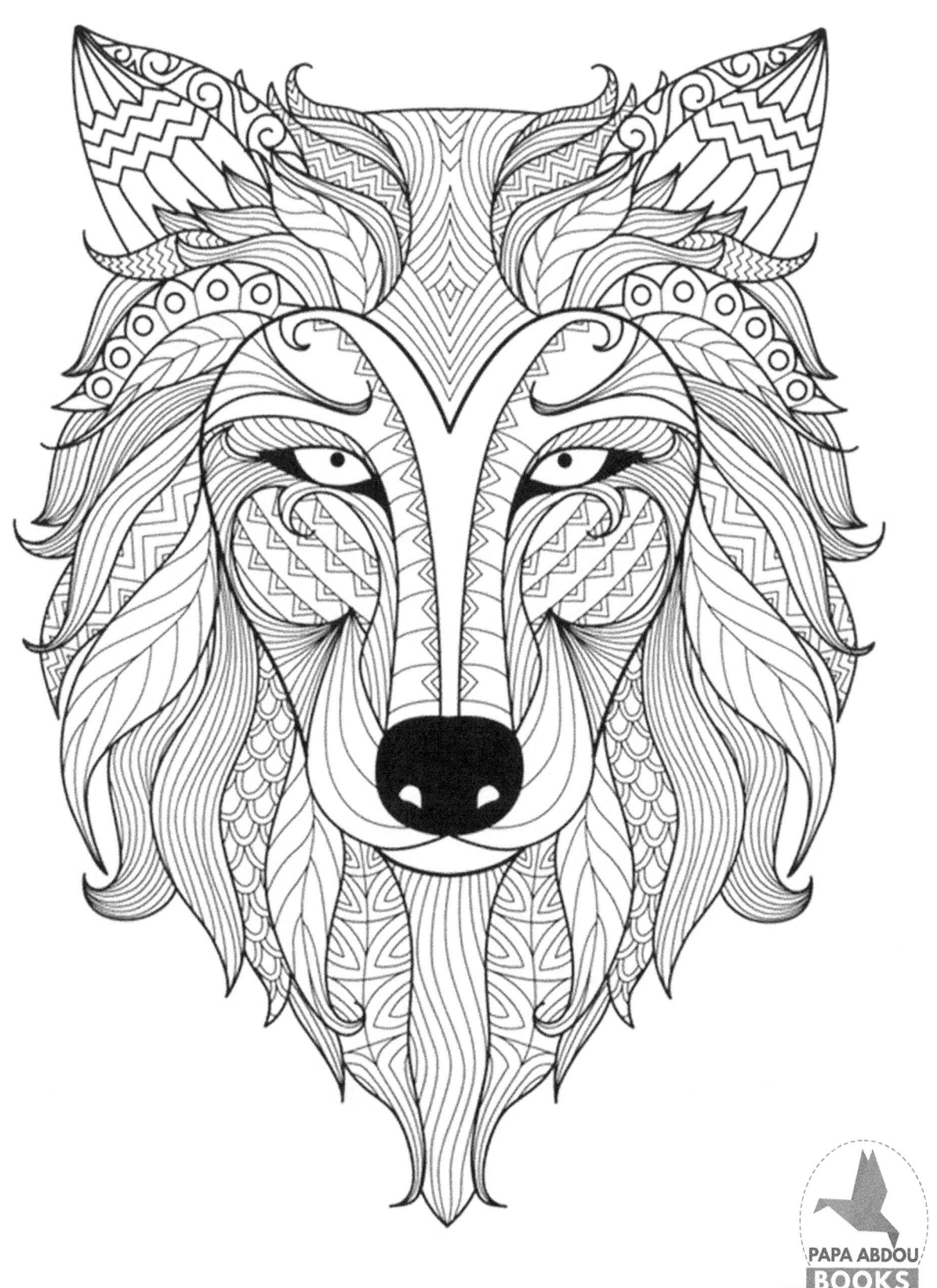

CopyRights 2020 Papa Abdou Books, Authour, Illustrator, or Publishing info.

www.ingramcontent.com/pod-product-compliance
Lightning Source LLC
Chambersburg PA
CBHW081700220526
45466CB00009B/2829